LIBERTY IN LEADERSHIP

A Workbook Study to A Healthy & Balanced Leadership Life

Debra E. Jordan

This book or parts thereof may not be reproduced in any form, stored in retrieval system, or transmitted in any form by any means – electronic, mechanical, photocopy, recording, or otherwise – without prior written permission of the publisher, except as provided by the United States of America copyright law.

Unless otherwise noted, all Scripture quotations are from the New King James Version of the Bible. Copyright 1979, 1980, 1982 by Thomas Nelson, Inc., publishers. Used by permission.

Scripture quotations from the Classic Amplified Bible. Old Testament copyright 1965, 1987 by the Zondervan Corporation. The Classic Amplified New Testament copyright 1954, 1958, 1987 by the Lockman Foundation. Used by permission. All rights reserved.

Scripture quotations the Holy Bible, New Living Translation, copyright 1996, 2004, 2007. Used by permission of Tyndale House Publishers, Inc., Wheaton, IL 60189. All rights reserved.

Scripture quotations are from the Holy Bible, Good New Translation copyright 1966, 1967, 1970, 1971, 1976 1979, 1992 by American Bible Society, Harper Collins. All rights reserved.

Scripture quotations from the Message Bible, copyright 1993, 1994, 1996, 2000, 2001, 2002 by Eugene H. Peterson. Used by permission of Tyndale House Publishers, Inc. All rights reserved.

Copyright © 2021 by Debra E. Jordan

All rights reserved

DEDICATION

To my husband Randall and two beautiful daughters, Jessica and Janai:

With every word that I wrote, I was reminded of what is most important in my life as a leader. There is no greater joy in my life than you. You are God's gifts to me. Your support of love, encouragement, and laughter allows me to lead as a healthy leader. This has empowered me to step up and write this book to other leaders. I am blessed to call you my precious family treasures.

Contents

Dedication	iii
Foreword	vii
Acknowledgements	ix
Introduction	xi
Chapter 1 First Things First	1
Chapter 2 Look! Can You See I'm Broken?	8
Chapter 3 Character Building	18
Chapter 4 Liberty	25
Chapter 5 Accountability	35
Chapter 6 Superman/Superwoman Mentality	44
Chapter 7 Stress-Less	56
Chapter 8 Forgiveness After Failure	67
Chapter 9 Joy, The Key to Finishing Your Race	76
Conclusion	86
About the Author	87
Notes	88

FOREWORD

God works in mysterious ways. I have been a clinical psychologist for almost 30 years. In that time, I have supervised my fair share of students, all of them seeking degrees that require that they obtain supervision hours working under a licensed professional. I have always enjoyed helping and teaching, and I rarely turn down the opportunity. I met the author of this book, Ms. Debra Jordan, a few years ago when she contacted me seeking to have a senior mentor. I was confused, you already have your certification. I had never met anyone who wanted to do *more* hours of supervision than their degree had required. What a rare person! Ms. Jordan explained that she was in the habit of seeking out the wisdom and guidance of senior professionals for mentorship, and that she had recently lost her beloved elder mentor. I said yes to her request. And, as God works in mysterious ways, I now know that the mentee was sent to be the mentor.

Ms. Jordan is an experienced leader who recognizes and writes to the leader in all of us. She has developed foundational habits, practices, or disciplines that she shares to help leaders experience liberty and joy in their leadership roles. I now understand why she was in the habit of seeking mentors. She practices what she teaches about the importance of accountability, continual growth, and self-care.

Ms. Jordan's new book, *Liberty In Leadership* is based in scriptural teaching and I view it as a God-send. I have a library filled with books about psychology, religion, business, self-help. This book still managed to teach, encourage, inspire, and challenge me. *Liberty in Leadership* is an excellent resource for individuals and groups who want to explore their experiences as leaders. The book includes application tools such as self-exams, personal action steps, and group discussion questions. In reading and doing the book's Self-Exam questions, I identified habits or practices in my life that needed, as Ms. Jordan, calls it, "recalibration". I look forward to adding this book to my library and to sharing it with my clients.

We live in a world that often seems to be in desperate need of leadership. We see leaders burn out. We see people shy away from leadership. We see leaders disappoint or lose their way. Ms. Jordan has written *Liberty In Leadership* as a loving and restorative guide for leaders. It is a guide back to fundamental truth about leadership, a truth that is key to success.

B. Lynn Wadelton, Ph.D.
Lic. Clinical Psychologist

ACKNOWLEDGEMENTS

A special thank you to my spiritual parents, Bishop George and Pastor April Davis. Thank you for your love, your example of leadership, your support, and for being the best Pastors and teachers of the Word of God to me. You encouraged me to share what God has placed inside of me with others to help them grow and develop as leaders. It is a privilege and honor to be a part of your staff and congregation. I love you both.

In loving memory of my mentor and friend, Dr. Gloria Kennedy. She shared her experience and educational guidance as a Christian Clinical Psychologist and professor to help me move forward in my purpose. The times of fellowship and spiritual deposits will forever be cherished.

Thank you to Dr. Lynn Wadelton for agreeing to become my mentor. You continue to deposit and teach me so much pertaining to the field of Christian counseling. I can never say thank you enough for the hours that you spent listening to me share my heart concerning completing this project.

Thank you to my Small Group family. I am so blessed to have you in my life. We know God connected us for years in a very special way. You have inspired me more than you know to be the leader that God has equipped me to be. I am overjoyed to be a part of the impact that each of you are making in this world. It was easy for me to write these life lessons for others when I could see the way they inspired each of you to strive to be better leaders in your areas of influence.

A special thank you to the Impact Counseling team. I have been honored to lead a wonderful group of men and women for over 14 years. Each of you inspire me in your own ways to be intentional to live as a healthy leader in my life which allows me to be my best for you. You are the best team to do life with. Leading you is a joy and one that I will never take for granted!

Thank you to Dr. Andrea Hart and J. Nicole Warren for your assistance with editing and encouraging me to release this publication. Keep allowing God to use you to help others fulfill their God-given purpose as authors.

INTRODUCTION

I can recall growing up and being in school and being given many opportunities to stand before my peers. There were times when I would be asked to be the voice of a group project, or to share the concerns of the class to the teacher. I was not always interested or comfortable being out in the front and speaking to others. It was during the times that I would say no to an opportunity that my teacher would say to me "you are a leader". I wish I could tell you that those words made such an impression on me that I never resisted the urge to decline to lead again, but they did not. It was not until several years after high school that I began to embrace the gifts that God placed on the inside of me to lead others.

Your story may not be like mine, but I am sure you can recall the times during your life when you were exercising your leadership skills without an awareness that you were leading.

When we think about the word leadership, our minds tend to think of those who lead on the world stage such as political leaders, entrepreneurs, entertainers, sports professionals, military, medical and law enforcement leaders. The truth is that leadership is not exclusive to these individuals. If we take a look within, we will discover that there is a leader within each one of us waiting to be released.

Many people pursue various types of leadership. Others find themselves in leadership roles by chance. You may be in one of those groups. Whether you dreamed of being a leader as a youth, or found yourself in a leadership role by default, there is a mentality that each of us can tap into as a leader that is a key component of success. That mentality is called liberty.

Liberty in its simplest form is freedom. It is a place of operating without restrictions. If you look at most successful leaders, they have broken outside the boundaries of the ordinary and pursued something more.

Leaders who operate with most of the following are typically influential leaders:
- a clear understanding of their purpose
- authority
- vision
- courage
- influence in the lives of others
- ability to lead others
- a refusal to quit

These leaders demonstrate a never quit attitude in the face of obstacles or adversities. These individuals have a confidence in who they are as a person, and what their purpose is for being in a leadership role. However, even with all of these factors present, is this enough to guarantee liberty as a leader?

The purpose of the following pages is to allow you to examine your own life as a leader and learn how to truly impact the lives of those that you are privileged to lead. No leader can be successful in their role without first being successful in their personal life. A foundational truth to being a great leader is to first be a great follower. The Christian leader has the most famous example available to mankind in Jesus. The freedom or the liberty that Christians receive from a life in Christ motivates us through love to freely serve others. This may seem contrary to what the world around us portrays as they lead their businesses and families. As you read the following chapters do a history check of the leaders who finished their course with joy and those who failed. Research who influenced the steps of their leadership. What you will find is the leaders who followed Christ operated in liberty and succeeded in fulfilling their leadership call because they found their liberty in Christ.

My hope in writing this workbook is for this information to cause you to slow down and make sure that your relationship with Jesus Christ is growing deeper and stronger every day. In this book I invite you as a leader to take a good look inside your heart and your life to check the conditions of both as you lead others. I want to help you lead from a place of peace, joy, and fortitude as a leader; not from a place of brokenness that causes you to be tempted to quit every other day.

I will challenge you to examine whether you are still carrying out the assignment of God or have drifted off course to do your own thing. This book is designed as a resource to strengthen you in areas that are not as healthy as they could be and to encourage you to go higher in those areas that are bringing *glory* and *honor* to God.

Your purpose as a leader, your lifestyle as a leader, and your liberty to do all that you have been assigned to do has lasting impacts on everyone you lead. Therefore, let's take a closer look together at how we can experience liberty in leadership as healthy leaders.

This book includes these tools to aid you in healthy leadership practices:

- Personal Self-examination Questions
- Group Discussion Questions
- Scriptures for Reflections
- Special Prayers

Chapter 1

FIRST THINGS FIRST

Seek the Kingdom of God above all else, and live righteously, and he will give you everything you need.

— *Matthew 6:33*

WHAT MAKES A GOOD LEADER?

Many of us have heard the question "what makes a good leader?" The usual responses range from being brought up in a family of wealth and influence to attending the right college or university. Whatever the world believes is the best foundation for preparing a leader in society today, if it does not include an intimate relationship with God, then it is not a solid foundation. Without this foundational relationship with God, a leader will never be able to operate in liberty through the grace that a relationship with God provides.

The Apostle Paul tells us that in 1 Corinthians 15:10;

> *"But by grace of God I am what I am: and his grace which was bestowed upon me was not in vain; but I laboured more abundantly than they all: yet not I, but the grace of God which was with me"*

Paul understood that what he accomplished was not because of him, but it was God doing the work through him by God's Grace. God is the one that has the plan and the purpose for our lives, and He is the one that will help us to do it with joy.

THE SELF-EXAM

The first step that leaders must incorporate into their lives in order to keep God first place is in the area of self-checkups. Living a life of self-examination allows you to keep your focus on God rather than on yourself. A true self-exam brings you back to a place of recognition that you can do nothing without God. You are then open to see the areas in life where you have stepped ahead of God, left God out, or where God is moving right now.

Leaders always want to make sure that they are still in-tune with God and that He is still ordering their steps. God is the one who orders man's steps. He is the director of whatever assignment you are blessed to be able to participate in. The moment you start operating as if you know it all and no longer need to acknowledge God, you have just started down a path of disorder. This means that He is no longer first place in your assignment as a leader. It may also mean that God is no longer first place in your life, rather your own agenda is now first place. You can never separate from the vine or the source of your existence. He has to stay first place in your life.

THE FOCUS POSITION

The next step of importance regarding keeping God first place in your daily life as a leader is ensuring that you never get to the place where the focus of life is on doing the assignment that God has given rather than on God Himself. Your mind must be set on things above. God's ways must be executed above everything that you think or even desire to see come to pass in your life. It comes down to committing your way to God and trusting God to bring to pass all that is needful in order to fulfill your leadership purpose in life.

As a leader, you can never get to the place wherein you believe it is no longer necessary to seek God or His wisdom to carry out your assignment. When you neglect to seek God, this opens the door for distractions and frustrations to come into your life.

Distractions will always come to try to get your focus off of what God has told you to do. However, the distraction is not bigger than

God. God gives a promise in His Word regarding the truth about distractions and how to have perfect peace when they come. He tells us that tribulations, trials, distresses, and frustrations will come, but we are to be of good cheer because He has already conquered this world.

Keeping God first place reminds you that no matter what attempts to come up against you, it won't be able to defeat you or stop the assignment that He is allowing you to carry out as His leader. Never forget that the distractions of life that you allow to take precedence, or go unchecked in your mind, will shipwreck what God has ordained for your life as a leader.

THE FIRST PLACE POSITION

Finally, the most important element in keeping God first in your life as a leader means that you can never stop spending quality time in prayer on a daily basis with God. Jesus kept the Father first place in everything he did. He spent quality time in prayer daily. He pulled away from events, disciples, and even pressed beyond his fatigue to spend quality time with God. As we look to Jesus' example, we can clearly see that His prayer time allowed Him to complete all that God ordained for His life.

When we spend quality time in the presence of the Father a great exchange takes place. We are able to receive the heart of God. He fills us up in His presence and positions us to be poured out daily to those we lead. We in turn give Him all of our cares and worries about our life and our roles as leaders.

RECALIBRATE

How are you leading today? Are you trying to come up with your own plan? Have you become distracted or frustrated with how things are going in your leadership role? If you answered yes to either of those questions, maybe taking a moment to recalibrate is just what you need. We recalibrate when we spend time in God's presence. Yes, we are talented enough to come up with some good plans, but you and I don't want a good plan, we want God's plan. The only way we will ever know what He wants us to do is by spending time with Him daily. Let this mindset be your foundation for your role as a leader: Everything I do starts with God in prayer. This brings liberty in leadership.

PRAYER:

> *Heavenly Father, I know that I am unable to accomplish anything without you. As I prepare for this day, open my heart to receive your direction in everything that I will encounter today as I carry out your assignment. May my leadership cause others to desire a relationship with you. In Jesus Name, Amen.*

APPLICATION TOOLS:

Complete the self-examination questions to see if there are areas that you have put something else in the place of Jesus in your life.

SELF-EXAM QUESTIONS

1. Am I still seeking to fall deeper and deeper in love with God every day?

2. Do I think to ask God first about decisions concerning my calling; or do I pray after my plan does not work out.

3. Am I willing to make the adjustments to my schedule to allow me to keep God's order in my life?

4. Am I more concerned about my position or plans as a leader than my relationship with God?

5. Am I ready to set appropriate boundaries in my life to maintain an intimate relationship with God?

GROUP DISCUSSION QUESTIONS

Let's talk about what our personal and work lives really look like.

1. Do I have a healthy prayer life?

2. Do I read my Bible consistently?

3. Do I approach the Word of God openly, or do I approach it with an "I already know it" attitude? Would you say that the Word has become common to you?

4. Have you allowed others to be first place in your life before God?

5. Have I become a workaholic?

6. Are you still doing exactly what God directed you to do in your assignment as a leader?

Scriptures for Reflection: 1 Corinthians 15:10; Psalm 37:23; John 15:5; Colossians 3:2; John 16:33; Ephesians 3:19; Psalm 16:11; Proverbs 14:12; John 4:34

CONVERSATIONS WITH GOD (NOTES):

Chapter 2

LOOK! CAN YOU SEE I'M BROKEN?

Beloved, I pray that you prosper in all things and be in health, just as your soul prospers.

— 3 John 2

As we live out this life that we have in Christ, we can never lose focus that Jesus came so that we could have an abundant life. If something is operating in abundance then it is full, plentiful, and it is overflowing. Overflowing is of God. However, in order to get to a state of overflow the container cannot be cracked, broken or already full of something else. When you think about the word broken what comes to mind? When I reflect on the word broken, I think of words like separated, weak, not sound, empty. These words indicate to me that there is no way we will be able to contain anything on the inside, good or bad, without repairing the cracks and strengthening the weaknesses in our lives. Cracks are areas of brokenness that causes whatever is being placed inside to quickly, or even slowly, leak out. As leaders, if we find ourselves broken it should be our goal to allow God to do whatever is needful to bring us back to a place of wholeness not solely for us, but for those that we lead.

YOU ARE A DISPENSER

When we are called to be leaders we are called to dispense. Whatever is on the inside of us in full capacity will always come out. Notice I used the words full capacity. It does not matter what character trait this may be, if it is operating at full capacity in our lives it will manifest in our positions as leaders. This includes those broken areas.

Our character is demonstrated on a daily basis. As a Christian leader we should strive to allow our character to reflect that of Christ. Our reaction and responses to situations will display whether we have. areas of negativity, low self-esteem, anger, bitterness, unforgiveness, or self-centeredness operating in our lives. These are all negative traits that require us to seek God for healing. If not dealt with, at some point they will begin to disperse on a daily basis whether we are aware of it or not.

NEGATIVE TRAITS
- *Negativity*
- *Low self-esteem*
- *Anger*
- *Bitterness*
- *Unforgiveness*
- *Self-centeredness*

Let's stop for a moment to reflect and search our hearts to see what is really on the inside. Are you hiding your heart behind your drive to become the super leader of your department? Have you found yourself always saying yes to compensate for feelings of low self-esteem? Here is one that I can personally relate to, are you refusing to deal with bitterness and unforgiveness towards someone who hurt you from your past that you no longer recognize who you are? It is time to get honest with yourself about the broken areas that have been hidden deep on the inside. Your life, or I could say the quality of your life, depends on you no longer ignoring the pain in the depth of your heart.

BROKENNESS

Acknowledging brokenness is a tough reality that is often difficult to deal with by many, especially those in leadership. No leader wants to believe that there may be an area or even areas in their life that is not whole. Most leaders spend their lives putting band-aids on the areas that have been broken in the past with the thought that ignoring them means that they are no longer issues.

For the purpose of this study, my working definition of the word brokenness is when we have anything in our lives that has been fractured, torn apart, pieced, or wounded. If you are like me there have been areas in life over the years that were described exactly that way. There is no shame in saying that I don't have it all together. It is quite the opposite. Acknowledging that there are areas of brokenness to yourself first and then being willing to invite God and others whom you trust to help you, demonstrates courage and strength.

In and of ourselves, we do not have the ability to bring complete wholeness back into our hearts. However, when we submit these areas to God and cooperate with His love and guidance, He brings us back to that place of nothing missing and nothing broken. If we had the ability to heal ourselves, God would never have needed to send Jesus to do it.

> *He heals the brokenhearted and binds up their wounds.*
> *— Psalm 147:3*

Oftentimes as leaders there is a deception that because we continue to complete our assignments well, function at a high level, and do multiple activities at the same time, that we must have it all together. I want to pause and give you an analogy to help you to further understand this deception. Picture a piece of fruit and envision displaying the fruit as perfect due to its appearance on the outside. The reality of the condition of the fruit is not known until you open it up. On the inside this fruit is rotten, smelly, spoiled, and bitter because it was not stored and cared for properly. The same is true for us as individuals. We can be doing everything well, saying all of the right words and looking clean on the outside, but on the inside, we are fractured, bitter and broken.

If we have not allowed God to care for us properly and heal our fractured pieces, we are attempting to lead others from a place that has cracks. Yes, life will come and hit you hard sometimes leaving broken pieces of the pain. This doesn't mean that you are not strong or that you are incompetent. No, it means that something entered into your life, and you have someone to turn to for restoration.

We can be healed from the pain of our past and then allow what we display to others to be an authentic testimony that God can restore us to a place of wholeness.

MULTI-TASKING, IS IT REALLY A GOOD THING?

Multi-tasking is a tool that the enemy uses to burn us out and keep us distracted. As a leader in today's society if you are not doing at least six to seven things at one time, some will view you as not giving your all. When we get to the bottom line of the effects of multi-tasking it simply means that you are living in a state of constant overload and pressure. This can cause things to break down in your life. In most cases, doing a lot of things simply means that you are not excelling in anything.

> **Multi-tasking** *is a tool that the enemy uses to burn us out and keep us distracted.*

The other factor involved in multi-tasking that many do not consider is that it brings a level of stress along with it. Stress will always have negative impacts in our lives, and it will take away the ability for us to walk in a place of tranquility. Stress opens the door for many emotional behaviors such as worry, frustration, anxiety, and a number of physical symptoms that will cause our bodies to break down. If we are not able to maintain a healthy life, we won't be able to lead anyone if we end up in a hospital bed or the grave. The Bible gives us a good formula for how to avoid stress. If you have never taken advantage of this, decide to do so today. I share more on the topic of stress in a later chapter.

> *Casting the whole of your care, all your anxieties, all your worries, all your concerns, once and for all on Him, for He cares for you affectionately and cares about you watchfully.*
> *— 1 Peter 5:7*

IS YOUR SOUL CRYING?

Our soul pertains to our mind, will, and emotions. It is within these areas that brokenness can occur and also be disguised. These three factors play a huge role in our lives, and they must be governed by something more than each other. Think about it, our mind gets ideas and directions from all types of sources whether good or bad. If we solely rely on our thinking to guide our lives, we will have some challenges. Our will is tied to what our mind and our emotions are directing it to do. Our emotions are designed to move us into motion, which is typically in the direction that our mind and will are leading. The problem comes when our soul is unhealthy, and we refuse to acknowledge it and continue to operate under the guise that all is well.

If there is an area in your life where you feel the effects of hurt, pain, failure, and disappointment, it will be in your soul. A broken soul means that every area of your life will begin to fracture, and it is just a matter of time before what is happening in your soul affects your physical bodies and every area of your life. Yes, you can mask these emotions for a period of time and even continue to function and be productive in your role as a leader. Eventually your brokenness will begin to show and cause you to change how you lead others.

The way to keep your soul healthy is by having a relationship with God, renewing your mind through God's Word, and establishing healthy relationships with others.

A part of being a good leader requires that you keep learning, growing, and developing in every area of your life. This involves more than natural lessons; it requires spiritual lessons. Learning to take care of your soul is a spiritual lesson. Learning to acknowledge the condition of your heart to an all-knowing God is a spiritual lesson. Admitting when your mind is full of negative thoughts that have damaged your emotions and caused your will to be out of line with the will of God for your life is a spiritual lesson.

> *A part of being* a good leader *requires that you keep learning, growing, and developing in every are of your life.*

How do you go about developing a habit of learning the condition of your soul? Where do you begin? As previously stated, having an intimate relationship with God through a life of prayer and worship, along with doing self-examinations are essential. God will tell you what things you should be focused on daily which will close the door to pressure and stress. He will enlighten you to areas of potential danger in our lives that if they are not brought into balance could cause things to break. He will teach you how to listen to His promptings and direction to start the healing process in your soul and the pathway to wholeness in areas that are broken.

Once you have identified the areas of brokenness that you believe need to be submitted to God, allow Him to show you what adjustments to make. Surrender it all to God by handing it over on Him even if the pain of the past is trying to speak louder than the promise of your future. If your soul is crying out in pain, refuse to settle in the land of cracks and broken pieces. You must decide to renew your mind with God's healing power and love for you.

There is something that happens in your mind when you are able to get the right perspectives in your heart. God's love is the right perspective. It will cause you to begin taking the steps to allow Him to heal the wounds in your soul and allow you to lead from a healthy place.

As a leader, you must know your vulnerable spots in your life and keep borders around them. Ask God to show you what boundaries are necessary to continue your assignment as a leader in your personal and professional life. You won't regret it and you will no longer have to say that you are broken. Instead, you can help others find their wholeness in God as they begin to lead others.

APPLICATION TOOLS:

Complete the self-examination questions to see if there are areas where Soul Care is needed that you have not acknowledged.

SELF-EXAM QUESTIONS

1. Are there broken areas in your life that you have not yielded to God?

2. How have these broken areas impacted your ability to grow as a leader?

3. Have these secrets hindered those that you lead from receiving more from you because you are afraid to be transparent with them as their leader?

4. Are there any open doors in your life that could be allowing you to keep nurturing your broken wounds?

5. Can you identify any negative traits in your personality that you are nurturing?

GROUP DISCUSSION QUESTIONS

1. Have there ever been times in your life as a leader that you felt frustrated, anxious, or even full of tension? Share what that was like for you.

2. What affect did it have on you personally?

3. What affect did it have on other relationships in your life? Business and personal.

4. What are the disadvantages of continuing to operate as a leader with brokenness in your life from past hurt and pain?

5. How can you implement **Soul Care** (*protection of your mind/will/emotions*) into your daily life?

Scriptures for Reflection: 1 Peter 5:6-7; Psalm 139:1; Psalm 139:23; Proverbs 20:27; Psalm 147:3; Isaiah 61:1; Psalm 107:20; 3 John 1:2; Romans 12:2

CONVERSATIONS WITH GOD (NOTES):

Chapter 3

CHARACTER BUILDING

Search me thoroughly, O God, and know my heart! Try me and know my thoughts! And see if there is any wicked or hurtful way in me, and lead me in the way everlasting.

— Psalm 139:23-24

WHAT'S IN A CHARACTER?

True leaders, specifically Christian leaders, possess quality character traits which can have a great impact on those that they lead. Whether you have found yourself leading in your family, school, church, or corporation, there are tools that can help you go to your next level in leadership. Strong, effective, leadership begins with a solid foundation. For a Christian leader, our character building has its foundation in living a life that imitates Jesus Christ.

A person's character is seen and established by what he/she does consistently over a period of time, especially when under pressure. The truth is that whatever is on the inside of you in abundance is what will manifest in overflow on the outside. This means that no matter how you attempt to disguise who you are, whatever is on the inside of you in abundance will come rushing forth on a consistent basis. Motives, actions, words, attitudes, and even brokenness will be seen by those that we have an opportunity to lead. At the same time, a pure heart, love, joy, peace, goodness, gentleness, faithfulness, longsuffering, temperance, and meekness can also be seen.

THE CHRISTIAN LEADER

As we take a closer look into the foundational truths of a Christian leader, we have to understand the makeup of the Christian leader. The Bible states that man was made in the image and likeness of God. It also states that Christians have been made the righteousness of God through Christ. Therefore, when you understand that as a Christian leader you are righteous, it should be a natural character trait that others are able to see on a consistent basis. Notice, I did not say as a Christian leader you will be perfect. I am saying that God's DNA on the inside of you as a Christian should compel you to display character traits that make it evident that you have been made the righteousness of Christ as you lead.

If there are areas that you are thinking of as you read this that you feel are not looking like Christ, you always have the ability to do something about changing what you see. You do this by asking God to help you in those areas to allow for growth to take place.

You may be asking, "What does righteousness look like for me as a Christian leader"? Is it based on my appearance or my charisma? Some may believe that it is based on their title or educational background. Those traits and accomplishments have their place in your life, but they in no way reflect whether or not as a Christian leader you are operating in righteousness. In order to identify what righteous character traits look like for a Christian man or woman, we must always go back to the Word of God. This is our guidebook for character building.

CHARACTER TRAITS

The Bible states that one of the character traits displayed by a righteous man or woman is that person is *gracious*, meaning there is a presence about them that is so pleasant and inviting that others enjoy being around them. A righteous man or woman is *full of compassion*.

This trait is displayed when they are leading their teams or organizations in such a way that says they genuinely care about those that they are called to lead. Their desire is always to see their co-workers and employees win. It is no longer about winning at the expense of others. They have an understanding that if those that they are leading are losing, then they are also losing.

A righteous leader is just that: *righteous*. This leader is just in their actions and fair in their handling of business matters.

> *The righteous leader is just that:* **righteous***.*

The righteous leader also *shows favor*, which means that they consistently extend favor to those that they lead, causing others to desire to work for them. Wow, wouldn't you like to be able to touch the lives of others with the favor of God to that degree where people are fighting to be on your team. The leader who shows favor to their employees shows *mercy* to them.

This type of leader is also a *lender*. Now immediately you may think that this is referring solely to lending money. But according to the Word of God when a righteous person is a lender, they are joining themselves to the other person. Can you image a leader who is so vested in their employees or organization that they truly become a part of every aspect of the success of those they lead? This is just something to ponder for a moment. Think about the lasting effects on an employee or co-worker who knew that no matter what, their leader was joined to them not just for what they brought to the company, but just because of who the leader was in Christ.

A righteous leader also has *good judgment* and *expects good things*. I don't know about you, but I surely want to be able to make wise decisions.

When we make wise decisions, we will always be in expectation of good things coming our way.

The last character trait that I would like to share with you regarding that of a righteous Christian leader is that their heart is *fixed on trusting God*. Out of all the character traits of the righteous Christian leader, being firm in your stance to trust God will solidify all of the other traits. This means that there is an unwavering confidence that God will complete in you what he started and will help you fulfill all that he has called you to do as a leader.

AN UNSHAKEABLE FOUNDATION

This is how you build your character as a leader and as a Christian. You build it on the foundation of your DNA as a son or daughter of God. It is unshakeable! Wouldn't you like to grow to allow others to experience God in your department or organization? It is possible and it starts with you!

Remember the goal is to walk in liberty as you lead. In other words, if it is necessary to dig everything up on the inside of your heart to ensure that the foundation is correct, then be willing to do just that. Taking time to pray and allow God to help you tweak some areas of your life will bring about character growth.

Don't resist the opportunity to grow. Resistance to development is resistance to growth, which ultimately leads to failure. Operating consistently in Godly character will always allow you to succeed.

APPLICATION TOOLS:

Examine your character as a leader and ask God to show you if there are any areas that He wants you to develop and grow.

SELF-EXAM QUESTIONS

1. How do I see my character as a leader?

2. Of the character traits I currently display as a leader, are there any areas where growth and change are needed? This applies to my personal and professional leadership life.

3. What steps can I take to allow me to continue growing and developing in my character as a leader?

4. Do I see growth in my character as an opportunity for growth for those I lead? If not, then why?

5. Is there any part of my character that I have refused to allow God to develop in my life?

GROUP DISCUSSION QUESTIONS

1. How can our character affect those that we lead?
2. Have you ever had to work for someone with questionable character traits? What was the result?
3. As a leader do you look for ways to help your team members develop in their character?
4. Do you see a difference between leading at home and leading at work? How can one affect the other?
5. How can your Godly character traits help you experience liberty in your leadership and as a Christian?

Scriptures for Reflection: Luke 6:45; Genesis 1:26; 2 Corinthians 5:21; Galatians 5:22-23; Philippians 1:6; Psalm 25:4-5; Psalm 86:15; Micah 6:8; Zechariah 7:8-10

CONVERSATIONS WITH GOD (NOTES):

Chapter 4

LIBERTY

So if the Son sets you free you are truly free.

— John 8:36

When God gives you the opportunity to function as a leader, there should be some evidence of freedom that comes along with this position because God is directing your steps. For a Christian leader there is no greater place of joy than to fulfill your God given purpose in life. This is contrary to what most individuals experience as they advance up the ministry or corporate level. We have a choice, whether to experience blessings rather than turmoil. Remember I said that liberty in its simplest form is freedom. The question then becomes what is the source of my freedom? I'm so glad you asked, let's take a closer look into this question.

THE SOURCE OF FREEDOM

There is only one reason that we are unable to operate in liberty in these positions, and it is the absence of the presence of God. When we are operating in purpose it is not a place of sorrow and toiling. It is a place of grace and growth; a place of joy and prosperity; a place of peace and health. This is God's plan for our lives.

Walking in liberty while working in leadership requires an understanding of the source of our liberty as Christian leaders. It requires a lifestyle of living in the presence of God. There is a beautiful promise in Psalm 16:11 which says, *"You will show me the way of life, granting me the joy of your presence and the pleasures of living with you forever.*" If God is showing us how to live, I believe that this includes our positions as leaders. I don't know about you, but I need God to show me how to experience liberty in my assignment as a leader. It is challenging to try to lead others on a daily basis with the weight of the world on your shoulders.

There are so many competing suggestions for leaders on how to be successful in the workplace. You can evaluate which one that you believe will help you accomplish the world's version of success. However, I want to offer you another suggestion and that is do not neglect abiding in God's presence for direction as a leader. As you ask Him to show you how to operate with ease in your role as a leader, it will allow you a level of freedom that you may not currently be experiencing. This is the secret to your success and your liberty in leadership.

BONDAGE

If you are not experiencing freedom in your role as a leader, you may be operating in bondage. I want you to understand that when I use the word bondage in this context, I am referring to any area of your leadership wherein you are allowing the assignment to control you. This would include areas wherein you view what you are doing and those that you are leading as obstacles and challenges, rather than opportunities to develop and disciple. We should always be leading from a place of freedom in order to allow those that we lead to flourish.

> *If you are not experiencing freedom in your role as a leader, you may be operating in* **bondage**.

Have you considered that if you are in bondage as a leader, those that you are leading and the area that you are overseeing may not be operating at its full potential? Your department or organization has probably maxed out because you are unable to take it further due to limitations in your own life. This applies not only to leading in business, but in your family and other relationships as well.

Let's say that you have been dealing with thoughts of failure, you better believe that your approach to the area that you are leading will reflect those thoughts. You find yourself playing it safe with projects and assignments in your area. I promise you that this mindset of failure will hinder every aspect of your leadership and relationships. You will always be afraid to step out and operate with boldness. Keep in mind, you have the ability to change the dynamics of this scenario. You can always ask God to show you what areas in your life are hindering you from being effective as a leader, and then decide to do the work to change. If you won't allow God to help you receive freedom it can hinder every relationship in your life and keep you from operating at maximum strength.

Remember, you will see change all around you when you tap into the source of your freedom, which is the presence of God. This is a benefit that we should not neglect.

THE BENEFITS

There are benefits to understanding the liberty that is available to us as Christians. This type of revelation helps leaders to understand that they are not responsible for the answers that are needful to be successful in their leadership role. Liberty is freedom! You are free to put down the agitations and worries at any time that come with being a leader. Notice that I said you can put these things down. In other words, it is a choice.

When you realize that you do not have to lead from a place of anxiety or confusion about the responsibilities that come with being a leader, it allows you to experience liberty while leading. It allows you freedom to be more transparent and encouraging to those that you are in relationship with as a leader and in your personal life.

> *"For I know the plans I have for you, says the Lord. They are plans for good and not for disaster, to give you a future and a hope."*
>
> — Jeremiah 29:11

The next benefit available to you when you operate in liberty is simply to enjoy the journey instead of feeling like you have to come up with all of the details for your position.

It is God's plan for you that you come to Him to receive wisdom to carry out His plan and purpose for your life on a daily basis. Not just when you feel that you are encountering something that is too big for you to handle. This means in every area of your life, including your responsibilities as a leader.

There are secrets and insights available for what your next month or next year will require. God will even show you how to be a greater influence on your employees and organization. He knows what processes and procedures need to be adjusted to allow you to be prepared for the demands of three years from now. He knows who you should select for a position before you even do a job post to fill the position. I don't know about you, but I am learning that it is easier to just ask God to show me how to lead. The toughest part for me has been learning how to wait patiently for God to answer my inquiries.

We live in a time wherein waiting on anything is something that no one desires to do, including me. If we are going to receive what God has for our lives, there will be times when we must wait on Him for the answers. When we wait on God, we experience His peace because we are so focused on Him and wanting to receive His help in our situation that the worry fades into the background. Remember God knows the plans He has for us, and since He does, He causes all things to work for our good in His wonderful purpose for our lives. Now that is a benefit worth waiting on.

Are you beginning to see that there is a far better way that is more beneficial to your organization and family when you implement the benefits that are available to you when you receive Jesus into your life? These benefits include your liberty!

WHEN I REFUSE

When we refuse to acknowledge God in our role as a leader, it takes away our ability to focus on others. Our modus operandi as a leader should represent the character of God in our workplaces. This statement is only true if you are a Christian who has decided to allow God to be the leader of your life.

You may want to ask yourself these questions about your leadership practices to determine if you are applying the benefits available to you as a Christian leader:

> - *Do you spend the majority of your time worrying about how to solve problems, or do you focus on helping your team grow and develop?*
> - *Are you so uptight about getting the assignments done or moving on to your next position that you cannot see your real purpose for being a leader?*

Time with God will not only make you a better leader, but it will also teach you how to serve others rather than be served. It will give you the liberty to demonstrate a Kingdom leadership style that is contrary to what we see in our world. It will allow you to become a better version of yourself as a leader. Who would not want the benefit of being a better version of themselves? I definitely would.

If you have not been experiencing liberty in your role as a leader it is not too late to start. Your willingness to submit your life to God, along with the adjustments that you are willing to make, opens up the possibilities to experience liberty as a leader. The wonderful part of this decision is that it is your choice to follow God's plan for leadership. However, the impact that your choice will have will be seen in the areas where you lead.

Refusing to apply the wisdom that God has given you as a leader will hinder your ability to operate in liberty, while at the same time you risk putting those that you lead in bondage. The bondage for your team members may come in the form of not receiving good direction or training from you as their leader.

When a team member is unable to be developed properly, it may cause the organization or department to suffer. The team member may lack the skills that would allow them to grow and develop as a leader. Your team needs for you to trust God by following His lead.

I want to leave you with the thought that you have a responsibility as a leader to choose liberty. Choosing liberty as a leader allows those under your leadership an opportunity to receive everything that God has for them from you. If you refuse to be free, others are affected. Choosing liberty today for you, your family, organization, and your team.

APPLICATION TOOLS:

Use the listed tools below to help you continue to walk in freedom as a leader.

PERSONAL ACTION STEPS

1. **Renew your mind.** *Read the Word of God regarding God's presence and role in your life as his son or daughter. Find out what type of leader Jesus was as He walked the earth. Learning to embrace who you are as a child of God first will allow you to start on a wonderful journey of a renewed mind of liberty in leadership.*

2. **Acknowledge God daily.** *Make it a part of your daily regiment to ask God for wisdom for the day. God cares about every aspect of your life and as you take the time to get direction for each day, each decision, each project, each problem, it will make for a better and more productive day.*

3. **Spend time in prayer.** *Living a life of prayer (which is communication with God) allows you to receive wisdom and guidance from God for every area of your life. You are able to give God those areas as a leader that are causing worry and frustration.*

4. **Never forget that it is God who will complete the assignment.** *Remind yourself that God birthed you for a purpose on this earth and that He will complete what He started. He is working in and with you to grow and develop you in every area of your life, including your role as a leader.*

Prayer:

Heavenly Father, in the Name of Jesus, I pray that as I acknowledge you in all of my ways you have promised to direct my paths. I know that as I spend time in your Word daily my mind will be renewed allowing me to not be confirmed to this world, but to be transformed into what you have created me to be. As I take advantage of the ability to communicate in prayer with you daily, I will know your perfect will for my life as I lead others. Through knowing your will, it then allows me to have this confidence that because it is you who has begun this good work in me, it is you who will complete it. I submit my life and assignment as a leader to you. Show me what you desire of me. I thank you and rejoice today as I receive my liberty that comes from abiding in your presence in Jesus Name, Amen!

GROUP DISCUSSION QUESTIONS

1. Have you ever applied for a leadership position because you needed to get it on your resume to help you qualify for another leadership role?

2. What does freedom look like to you in your personal life and in your role as a leader?

3. Have you ever felt as though you were in bondage to your past?

4. Is there anything in your life today that could hinder you from leading from a place of freedom?

5. What could you commit to add to your life today to help you experience liberty as you lead?

Scriptures for Reflections: Romans 12:2; Psalm 16:11; Proverbs 3:5-6; Jude 20; Jeremiah 29:11-12; Romans 8:28; Philippians 1:6

CONVERSATIONS WITH GOD (NOTES):

Chapter 5

ACCOUNTABILITY

A friend loves at all times, And a brother is born for adversity.

— *Proverbs 17:17*

WHO IS ON YOUR SIDE?

Accountability is necessary to the success of life whether you are a leader or not. Just think for a moment about the people who have been in your life who have watched you take your first job to seeing you as a leader today. Would you say that they have added some positive benefits to your life? Having someone in your life to stand with you, pray with you, encourage you, and yes, even correct you is necessary, especially in leadership.

It has been said that the higher you go in leadership the lonelier it gets. I don't necessarily agree that it gets lonelier, I believe that God will sometimes shift the crowds along our journey in life to bring others in for that season. Having those special people in our lives at pivotal moments can make all the difference in the world. Sometimes having the right people in our lives can actually save our lives. We don't ever want to be alone when the trials of life come up against us. You may wonder why I made this statement. Allow me to explain further.

Anytime we find ourselves alone when life hits hard, it puts us in an unprotected position. I want you to picture a person standing on an island with nothing around them, this includes no animals, no trees, and no shelter. As you are reflecting on this image, I would like you to notice that because there is nothing or no one around the person to protect them, it doesn't matter what size of an object, the strength of the wind, or even the frequency of raindrops falling, the person is uncovered and unprotected on all sides. When we choose to live life alone, we look just like this person on the island. We position ourselves to be uncovered and unprotected.

You may have experienced hurt in a past relationship and this is causing you to be closed to letting others in your circle. Relationships can hurt because they are made up of imperfect people. We do not have to put so much pressure on others to be perfect when we recognize that we can be in a relationship with a perfect God. Our relationship with God is the only one that will never let us down and will cover us when we feel as though we have been let down by others. The more we understand this truth, it will allow us to stop putting so much pressure on others to be perfect before we are open to building relationships.

Don't ever get so caught up in business that you forget the importance of having others in your life. Everyone needs that person or persons who can speak into their life and love them enough to tell them the truth, even when it is difficult to say. Your accountability person may be your spouse, sibling, best friend, co-worker, or even a small group member. Whoever God leads into your life is there for a purpose. Never forget that a circle of Godly friends not only has the ability to save your life and career but can help propel you into a healthier level in your role as a leader. So, take a look at your life and see who is in your corner today. If there isn't anyone, it's time to open up and ask God to send you someone to begin developing your circle of friends.

TRUTH OR LIES?

What are some important factors for you to consider as you build your circle of accountability going forth? The first would be to allow these individuals to be comfortable saying to you as the leader that you are getting off track. They should not be afraid to tell you when you are wrong, or so insecure about themselves that they won't build you up when you need it.

Let's take for instance if you were praying about making a major change within your department or moving to another city, would you be able to seek counsel from them and know that they will not just tell you what you want to hear.

The second point to consider is will you be truthful with those who you have asked to hold you accountable. Can you honestly say that you are transparent in those relationships? Do these relationships allow you the ability to be comfortable sharing your secrets? If there is something that you are struggling to overcome, can you ask your accountability circle for help? All of these points are important to consider as you think of your circle of friends.

I previously asked the question whether your accountability circle would tell you the truth and not just what you want to hear. It is important for you to ask yourself will you be truthful with individuals in your life when you need to have a tough conversation? You may be wondering what all of this has to do with having liberty as you lead. The answer is everything. When we are not able to have authentic and healthy relationships in our lives, it leads to stress in our lives. It is always liberating when we speak the truth with those in our circle of close relationships. When we commit to operating this way first, as well as grow in our relationships, it will be easy for us to identify and receive the people that God has sent into our lives to be a part of our circle of accountability.

There are some basic character qualities that we can look for in others as we develop accountability relationships. These qualities include honesty, trustworthy, humility, transparency, integrity, love, and the ability to give and receive constructive correction. It is important for others to display these qualities, but it is just as important for you as a leader to possess them as well.

> **ACCOUNTABILITY QUALITIES**
> - *Ability to receive constructive correction*
> - *Honesty*
> - *Integrity*
> - *Trustworthy*
> - *Love*
> - *Transparency*
> - *Humility*

FIRE DAMAGE

A leader without accountability in their life is like the embers of a log fire. As long as someone is watchful, the embers provide what is necessary for enjoyment and comfort. Even if the flames began to blaze up again, with the right oversight and attention, it can quickly be brought back under control. However, if there is no one keeping a watch over the logs it can easily began to burn out of control and end up destroying everything in its path. Even to the point of total disaster. Did you ever notice that some house fires are so bad that nothing could be salvaged? An out-of-control leader can leave such devastation within their paths that lives are difficult to restore. A leader who is not willing to submit to God and others for accountability is operating on dangerous ground.

We have all seen leaders who fell from great heights, and it is never a pretty sight. We tend to question what the leader could have done to prevent this from happening. We wonder if there were people in the leader's life who failed to warn that danger was coming if correction was not made. It's easy to stand back and judge the leader in the spotlight, but my challenge to you is to judge yourself in this private moment to see if you are obeying God and listening to trusted friends in your life. When you surrender your life to God and allow others in for the purpose of accountability, it could be the difference between you healing in private or experiencing hurt and pain in public.

FOLLOW THE BLUEPRINT

If we have the right circle of friends in our corner, it can make a major difference for us in our successes and even our failures in life. The first relationship that is needful is the one we have with God. He is our first accountability and every other relationship that we have should be modeled after the one we have with Him. The Bible has a lot to say about relationships and the importance of them in our lives. Just think, God wanted to have a relationship with us so much that He gave us his only Son to connect with us.

As Christians, we understand that God is our number one accountability partner. He is with us at all times, and we can trust Him with the details of our lives. If we will seek His guidance to learn how to be a good friend, then it will be easy for us to identify individuals around us who could provide accountability for us. God allowed Jesus to set the example of how to lead in relationships and as a leader. All we need to do is imitate the blueprint given to us by God.

> *"Therefore be imitators of God copy Him and follow His example, as well-beloved children imitate their father."*
>
> — Ephesians 5:1

Experiencing liberty in leadership has more to do with you as the leader than the individuals you are called to lead. Taking this time to allow God to search your heart in this area of accountability could be the element that has been missing for you to experience liberty. Trust God to show you any area that may require some immediate attention. Then ask Him to show you how you can be a good accountability partner to someone else. Accountability does not involve shaming. Accountability is a safe place to experience freedom.

APPLICATION TOOLS:

Examine your life and be honest about the presence or absence of accountability relationships. Ask God to show you those individuals who could become your circle of friends.

SELF-EXAM QUESTIONS

1. Do you currently have a circle of friends in your life that you can be transparent with?

2. Have you been willing to open up to the people that God is sending in your life to be your circle of accountability?

3. Do you have a challenge being accountable to another person, including God?

4. Is there any area of your life that is off limits to God?

5. Are you willing to live your life in such a way that others could trust you as an accountability friend?

GROUP DISCUSSION QUESTIONS

1. Share with the group your description of an accountability friend.

2. Is there a character trait that is more important to you for someone that you are considering to be in your accountability circle? Share with the group why this is important.

3. Have you ever been offended with someone in your life who shared their perspective on an area of leadership where you did not perform at your best? How did that make you feel? Is that person still a part of your life?

4. Do you see God as an accountability source in your life? If not, what would it take for you to change your perspective and allow God into every area of your life to help you become a better leader? Be honest with your response.

5. Do you see God as Omniscient (all knowing) in your life?

Scriptures for Reflections: Psalms 139:23-24; Proverbs 20:24; Psalms 37:5-6; Mark 11:25-26; Ephesians 5:1

CONVERSATIONS WITH GOD (NOTES):

Chapter 6

SUPERMAN/SUPERWOMAN MENTALITY

Take my yoke and put it on you, and learn from me, because I am gentle and humble in spirit; and you will find rest.

— *Matthew 11:29*

WHERE IS MY SUPER SUIT?

All throughout the Bible and our history in society we have many examples of men and women who did extraordinary things as leaders. Some appeared to accomplish these tasks supernaturally without the assistance of others. In this chapter, let's take a moment to explore some myths surrounding the mentality of a healthy leader.

Many individuals in leadership believe that a sign of being a good leader is displayed by some of the following traits:

- Working very long hours (60-80 a week).
- Doing everything yourself and never asking for help.
- Thinking that everything has to be your idea.
- Believing that success begins with the letter "I".
- Consistently taking on multiple projects at one time.
- Never taking a lunch break, a day off, or a vacation.
- Not taking an opportunity to enjoy your position of leadership.

- Using the phrase "one day I will have time to".

In looking at the short list above, did you locate any traits that may be a part of your thought process for what makes one a good leader? I like to call the above examples the *"superman/superwoman mentality"*. Unfortunately, this mentality is not healthy for anyone, especially for a leader.

It is never wise for a leader to lead others with a *"I can do everything all by myself mentality"*. This mentality is unhealthy in every arena including business. The Christian leader with this mentality gives the appearance that depending on anyone for help, including God, is unnecessary to succeed. We must remember that as a leader we are influencing those that we lead on a daily basis. If our team or organization is looking to us for direction and an example, would we want to project the image that taking a vacation to be with our family is unwise? Living a balanced work life in order to maintain a healthy life is a good example to set. God rested from His work, and if He rested, I'm pretty sure we should also. Just consider the impact that a leader has on their team or organization when they don't appear to be happy about coming to work because of fatigue and burnout. I promise you the impact is not good. Your team is always watching you and as a leader you are always influencing.

PRIDE OF WORK

Having a *"superman/superwoman mentality"* can really be translated into one word. That word is pride. Pride for a Christian leader is like kryptonite to superman. It will destroy you slowly! Unlike superman wherein he knew the danger and impact that kryptonite could have on his life if he were exposed to it, most Christians don't understand the magnitude of what pride does in our lives. The Bible gives us clarity what happens when anyone operates in pride, a fall is imminent. The deception that you never need to rest your body; spend time with your spouse and children; or allow those who are a part of your team to help you; are all character traits of pride. If you operate with this mindset, it will destroy you, and it will hinder those that you lead to go higher.

When you become a leader, your focus must shift from yourself to those that you lead. Your team, organization, and family are depending on you to help them succeed in their lives. As you lead others your success is measured by the success of these individuals, which is contrary to the worldview that your success is completely about what you are able to accomplish personally in your role as a leader. Remember you are attempting to lead a team to victory and there is no letter "I" in the word team.

> *"Let each of you look out not only for his own interests, but also for the interest of others"*
> — Philippians 2:4

Leaders who operate with this unhealthy pride mentality set a tone for the office and team that goes beyond their office, it actually infiltrates the employee's life. The tone that is being set is the tone of pride and it will always bring the tune of strife along with it. Think about what happens when an employee is demanded to consistently neglect home and family to work mandatory long hours weekly. I'm sure you would agree that if they are married or a single parent that there will be problems in their relationships at home. This kind of overwork causes stress and other health issues as well.

There will always be employees and team members who believe that when their leader works 60-80 hours a week, it demonstrates a sign that the leader is committed and an overachiever. Some employees will strive to duplicate this type of behavior. However, I do not want you to be naive to believe that there are not some employees and team members who resent a leader that operates this way. Picture this, there are two or three employees on your team of eight who believe that spending every evening working at the office is how everyone should operate. The breakdown will start in the group when the other team members push back against working late hours every day or not being able to put in for the vacation that they have earned. Eventually there will be division within your team due to what may be seen as a lack of trust and commitment to the team from those who don't agree with this mentality. A mentality that was modeled by you as the leader.

We also have to consider that this type of scenario would not be complete without pointing out that the diminished trust between the team members. It could also reflect a diminished trust amongst those employees that do not agree with your work ethic as a leader. This is when you have to spend time with God as your leader to bring balance in your life and to your team.

How often have you heard it said that people do not care how much you know until they know how much you care. Abandoning the superman/superwoman mentality by setting a balanced work life and personal life as the leader demonstrates to your team members that you care about them and the people who enable them to work for and with you.

ATTITUDE MATTERS

We often say if we want to know the character of a man to look at his friends. I say if you want to know how far an organization or a department will rise, look at the leader. The leader sets the tone from the top. What type of atmosphere are you setting as a leader? Have you ever stopped to take a look around at the attitudes of those that you oversee? Do you see joyful, grateful attitudes in your office, or do you see begrudging and sad attitudes? This examination cannot be confined to the workplace. Take a look at your family and evaluate the attitudes and atmosphere that is displayed within your home.

As we lead others, we must stop and ask ourselves are we creating followers to operate with the same attitude that we exhibit on a daily basis? If the answer is yes, what type of attitude are you displaying? Is your attitude helping your family and employees live a healthier life because you are their leader, or is it taking years off of their lives? If you are working without ever taking time to refresh, to build strong family relationships, or to do something as simple as take a lunch break then you are showing those that you lead how to work and live with the wrong attitude. You are showing them how to operate in their purpose with the mindset that they have to work themselves into the ground in order to experience success in life. Actually, this type of attitude is what shortens our ability to lead for the long term. Are you comfortable influencing others to embrace this unhealthy behavior?

You may not be leading your team and organization with the attitude described above, but I would probably guess that there are some ways that you can improve to bring a better attitude to your leader experience. Instead of having a do-it-yourself superman/superwoman mentality, leaders should put themselves in a position to work in a way that demonstrates to the team that every team member is valued. I know that this is not the attitude of most leaders whose total focus maybe on how to get recognized or positioned for the next promotion.

As Christian leaders our attitude should be outward focused as we lead others. What does it actually mean to have an outward focused attitude? Well, the answer is easy, we simply do what Jesus did while leading others. He demonstrated over and over again that He was there to teach others the ways of the Kingdom of Heaven, not this world, so that they could live a good life. His examples were not just for those individuals in the Bible, His examples are for us today. The word that I want you to draw your attention to in those sentences is the word *others*. Jesus cared about others and so should we.

What makes a team great includes the wisdom, skills, and work ethic of the leader, however, it does not negate the contributions of every person on the team. Have you ever recalled what it was like for you prior to being promoted to a leader? I'm sure you had many suggestions and ideas about things that could add to your team. Were you given an opportunity to provide those suggestions? How did you feel as a result of your leader taking the time to listen to you? How did you feel if your voice was not heard? If you can recall how you felt, then I would encourage you to pay that forward with those that you lead.

For the Christian leader there is no need to go around acting like a superman or a superwoman to impress others. It is okay for your team to see that you do not have all of the answers, but that you are willing to seek the one who does have all of the answers, which is God. Your attitude as a leader should be that you are seeking, leaning, and trusting God in your role as a leader. This does not mean that you walk around your office all day with your Bible open and wearing a big "C" on your chest for Christian. It means that you demonstrate confidence in God in your attitude towards your assignments and how you interact with your teams and organization. Allow your team to see the peace that comes when you trust God for the answers.

Take a moment and reflect on what attitude you present when you first meet a new team member. Do you present as you are the *super* supervisor who can do everything? Do you display the atti-tude that even though it is nice to have a new member on the team, you really do not need any new members because you are there to do it all? I want to take this moment to say you may have never verbally stated these types of things, but your attitude is sometimes shown more often by what you do not say than by what you say. Attitudes matter and are seen and heard.

Our attitudes can speak at high volumes through our body language. Whether you have operated this way or not, it is still worth taking this time to check your heart as the leader of your team, organization, and family to make sure that no remnants of pride have crept into your life and affected the way you lead. The truth about pride is that it can be seen and demonstrated in our attitudes. I constantly check my heart as I purpose to keep my attitude in line with my relationship with God versus the things that may be taking place around me as a leader. This includes my successes. I have to remember that I can do nothing without God leading me and helping me every step of the way. Let's never forget that we should continue to be a welcoming leader whose sole purpose for being in this role is to help our team succeed.

DON'T FORGET TO ASK FOR HELP

Do you know what can be one of the most difficult things for a leader to do? It is to ask for help. Somewhere along the line the notion that asking for help is a sign of weakness has caused many to fail. As Christian leaders we have the ability to invite God into any situation in our lives. God wants to help us be effective, honest, and kind leaders. We do not have to go day in and day out being full of frustration to accomplish an assignment. Afterall, we said that God purposed us to operate in the role that we are currently working. If God truly purposed us to carry out the leadership role we are currently operating in, then God is well able to help us complete and succeed in this role.

When we allow God into our roles as leaders, God can put his super on our natural and we will be amazed at how easy and liberating it will become to operate at a maximum level as a successful leader. Many successful leaders tend to be A-type personalities and therefore operate at high levels in their roles. Don't fall into the trap of attempting to lead like those who do not have God in their lives. If you remember nothing else from this book, remember that you are called to be different in this world. You are called to be the light in this world.

As a leader who follows Christ, you have to follow his way of leading. Think about this, Jesus operated at a high level, but he never lost sight of who set the standard for the way He conducted his life as a leader. Jesus never displayed pride, a defeated attitude, or going days and years without asking God for guidance and help in His life. There are so many lessons that we can learn from the life of Jesus that will transform us to be greater leaders. We just need to be intentional about spending time in the Bible and in prayer to learn these lessons.

As stated at the beginning of this chapter, we have many examples of leaders who succeeded and even those who failed. For those leaders who were Christians, you can always trace the beginning of their failure back to where they stop allowing God to lead and direct their steps. Make a promise and declaration today that you will never stop asking God for His help, guidance, and will for your life as you lead others. I don't know about you, but I do not want to lead without God teaching me how to lead others in a way that helps them be better in their purpose because I was their leader.

I'M HERE TO HELP

I know in this chapter I have shared with you some of the traps about getting lost in trying to do everything on your own as a leader without asking for help. It is never a sign of strength when a leader uses the world's approach of leading by saying I can be successful without the help of others around me. The greatest display of strength and power as a leader is when you are willing to make helping those that you lead succeed. It takes putting God's way for your team to succeed over accomplishing your assignments of the department or organization.

As a leader, when you serve others that you are called to lead, it develops trust and relationships. When you develop relationships, it is then easy to become transparent. A part of that transparency is asking your team for help, but it also involves letting them know that you are there to help them when needed. These actions help with liberty as you lead.

Helping your team succeed starts with caring enough about each member of the team to make sure that their mental health is in a good place. Demonstrating care for your team members includes asking about how their family members are doing and just being there to listen to the team member and pray for them. Many leaders have failed to realize that when you care first about the wellness of those you lead and demonstrate that you want to help them live a blessed life, the production of the department and organization will be better.

It may be surprising to you but caring about others is a good way to demonstrate who you are as a leader. I am sure that this is very different from what you may have heard or experienced in the past concerning how a leader should lead. Leading involves caring and caring involves helping those that you lead to be successful in the best ways possible. You will never be successful in leading others if you are not first successful in caring about those that you lead.

Helping others means that you are modeling your work ethic and yes, even your Godly character traits to those that you lead. Remember your influence as a leader will bring positive and even negative results. Therefore, as a Christian leader strive to ensure that you are allowing a good, well balanced, joyful countenance to be what your team and organization sees. It doesn't matter what comes up against you as a leader, if you know and understand that you do not have to lead without the help of God, it will allow you to be free to help those that you lead and ultimately allow you to have liberty in your role as a leader.

As you consider the information in this chapter, I'm sure that you can see it is easy to get the mentality that you have to do everything yourself in order to carry out your assignment and fulfill your role as a leader. This mentality will zap your ability to experience liberty in leadership.

Today you can be the leader that says my strength comes from God and without Him I can do nothing. Do you want to experience this type of liberty in your leadership role right now, or do you want the bondage of doing everything yourself? Whether it is someone you know, or if you have found yourself operating with a superman/superwoman mentality, you can make a shift right now and change the course of your leadership journey. It is never too late to experience freedom while leading others.

APPLICATION TOOLS:

Examine your life and be honest about how you are currently operating as a leader. Ask God to show you areas in your leadership that you have not allowed him to be your source of help.

SELF-EXAM QUESTIONS

1. Are there any unhealthy superman/superwoman character traits that have attempted to show up in your role as a leader?

2. What do you believe demonstrates the strength of a leader?

3. What kind of attitude do you display as a leader?

4. Are your team members comfortable coming to you for help?

5. Can you say that you are still following the instructions that God gave you when you first began in your role as a leader? If not, what can you do to get back in line with His purpose for your life?

GROUP DISCUSSION QUESTIONS

1. How dangerous is it for a leader to stop trusting in God to help them fulfill their assignment as a leader? How can this impact their team or organization?

2. Why is it important for your team to trust you as their leader?

3. How can you demonstrate to those that you lead that you value their contributions to the team and organization?

4. When was the last time that you took a vacation? If it has been longer than 6 months, share with the group the reason you have not taken time off to refresh.

5. Why does your attitude matter as the leader of a team or organization?

Scriptures for Reflection: Jeremiah 33:3; Proverbs 16:18; John 15:1-5; Philippians 4:13; Psalms 37:5; Philippians 2:5-7

CONVERSATIONS WITH GOD (NOTES):

Chapter 7

STRESS-LESS

Don't worry about anything; instead, pray about everything. Tell God what you need, and thank him for all he has done.

— *Philippians 4:6*

This chapter builds on the previous chapters in helping you experience liberty. In order to have liberty in leadership, each of the topics addressed throughout this book are needed. As we start this chapter, let's take a deep breathe. I would like to invite you to explore and examine the characteristics of stress and the impact that it could have if you refuse to handle it properly. Living a stress-less life positions you to experience liberty in leadership.

STRESS, THE SILENT SYMPTOM

As a leader there is always the potential from time to time to experience different types of stress in your position. It is important to learn early on how to respond to the symptoms of stress in a way that allows you to stress-less. It requires you to operate with an awareness of the symptoms of stress and with some knowledge for how to live a balanced life, to keep stress from overtaking you.

The way to bring balance in life is to develop an intimate relationship with God. It is our relationship with Him that allows us to live in a way that when the stressors of life show up, we do not have to let them inside of us. Our relationship with God allows us to view the issues of life in a way that no matter what comes up it will not be viewed as the big one that will take us out.

What is stress and what does it look like in our lives? In most cases, it is commonly defined as pressure. Stress can creep into our lives and impact us mentally, emotionally, physically, and spiritually. It is like a silent invader that can attack a person's body and open the door for other health challenges. One of the characteristics that makes stress such a dangerous invader is that it can be present in our lives for years without us ever knowing it is there.

Stress can manifest in various ways in our bodies that can appear to be physical symptoms. There are many ways that leaders and people in general attempt to deal with stress. Some try to treat the symptoms of stress with caffeine, food, shopping, smoking and even drinking.

Stress can sometimes manifest itself in your life in the form of worry, frustration, anger and even anxiety. Have you ever experienced any moments of insomnia, headaches, stomach aches, chest pains or even eating complications to name a few? If so, did you have your physician ask you what was currently taking place in your life on a daily basis?

In most cases, we may not realize the impact that different events, relationships, and work situations are having on our physical bodies. Especially if we are worrying and running at maximum speed on a daily basis trying to be a superman or a superwoman. Be open to sharing with your physician the changes that are present in your personal and professional life, as there may be a small chance that these things are related to stress.

When we talk about stress, there is an assumption that it only shows up when there are bad things taking place in our lives. The truth is that stress can show up with your next level of promotion as a leader or with the purchase of a new home. There is the possibility of getting over into stress with the relocation to a new city or moving into a new office due to your new promotion.

Other areas that can bring stress into our lives include, but are not limited to, planning a wedding, the birth of a child, getting a new contract or opening up a new business. You can see that these are wonderful new seasons of life, but make no mistake each of these celebrations can bring with it stress if we do not respond to them correctly.

What will be your response to stress when it shows up in your life? Will you allow the situation that you face to dictate your response, or will you do what the Bible instructs you to do which is cast all the care over to God? You must understand that your response is very important. How you respond will allow you to either be able to live a stress-less life or be a leader who is constantly experiencing health challenges in your day-to-day responsibilities. As a Christian, you do not have to respond to stress the way that non-Christians respond. God is your stress regulator which means there is a better way to view and deal with stress.

> *God is your **stress regulator**.*

WHO IS IN YOUR CIRCLE?

Unfortunately, some individuals will pretend that stress is something that never enters into their lives. Could it be because a leader who says I am stressed, that he or she is seen as incapable? In some areas of our Christian culture if you say that something is wrong in your life, or that something is coming against you, it is viewed as not operating in faith. It can even look as if you may not be spending enough time in prayer. Therefore, you have individuals, especially leaders, who walk around pretending that nothing ever comes up against them which only causes their stress level to be even higher. This is why accountability circles in our lives are needed.

As discussed in the previous chapters, having people in your life as accountability friends will enable others to help you to see when stress is attempting to enter in your life. Even if you were not mindful that you were operating in stress, those individuals around you who know you and love you, will be able to see that the way you are behaving is different from your normal behavior. Your circle can help you regain balance and give you a place to share the things that are causing you stress. This can also be a place where you can choose to allow those in your circle to help you to return to the stress-less zone.

PRAYER AND WORSHIP, STRESS RELEASERS

For Christian leaders, we do not have to feel as though all of the responsibility for our lives and roles as leaders is riding solely on our shoulders. There is a place in the life of a Christian leader that will allow you to enter into what I like to call the *stress-less zone*. It starts with living a life of *prayer* and *worship*. These are powerful tools that you have in your hands that can be the difference between winning and losing. When we enter into prayer and worship it is like taking the weights of the day off of our backs and handing them up to a loving God. We then receive what feels like a cool refreshing and unexplainable peace from God. It is not automatic to experience this type of exchange just because you are a Christian leader. It requires you to decide to access it as a child of God through prayer and worship.

Prayer can help to bring balance in your life. Prayer, which is just having conversations with God, has to be intentional. It is not something that you do as a last resort. If you learn to make prayer a part of your daily life, you will find that when life is pressing you with something that may cause you to stress that you can always talk to God about the matter. I actually do not think I have the best words to describe my conversations with God about my concerns, hurts and disappointments. The reason I do not believe I have the best words to help you understand my experience when I approach God about my potential stressors, is because everything stands still as I talk to God. All of my worries disappear because I can only see God and nothing else. The challenge for me is to not take back the things that I just released to God once I step out of prayer.

Talking to God is one of the most precious gifts that is available to us as Christians. It is a place of safety and peace like none other. *If you are reading this book and have never asked God to come into your life and be your Savior, today you can. There is a simple prayer at the end of this chapter that you can pray to ask God to come into your life.* I promise you as you take this step, you will look at your life in the months and years ahead and it will be different for you as a leader, a family member, friend, and in any other area where stress was attempting to rule you.

Worship is the other weapon that can transform any moment in our lives from stress and chaos to a place of supernatural peace. Worship is not just singing a song; worship is how we lead as leaders. Worship is how we treat our spouse and children. Worship is how we operate in integrity and righteousness as we carry out our assignments.

The reason why all of these things are an act of worship is because when we worship, we are focused on God and nothing else. In everything we do, we are to do it as unto the Him. Worship allows us to enter into the presence of a loving God who cares about everything in our lives. Worship relieves the tensions of stress and the tormenting thoughts that what we are worrying about is going to be that way forever. Worship reminds us that God's love for us is more powerful than anything we are facing in this world.

If you will make prayer and worship a part of your life for one week and immerse yourself into seeking God above all other responsibilities, even your daily leadership position, you will never want to start your day off any other way. Are you ready to give prayer and worship a place in your life today? I promise that the peace you will experience will be life changing.

THE SECRET TO MY SUCCESS

Considering all of the information that was shared in this chapter, what should our approach and response be to stress in order to remain stress-less as leaders? Here are some suggestions to consider:

1. As a Christian leader who desires to remain in the stress-less

zone you must seek and trust God for direction. Be willing to obey what He is telling you to do even when it does not make sense to your mind. Remind yourself that if the current position is where God told you to be, then He knows everything that you will encounter and has already given you everything you need to be victorious.

2. You must have a consistent prayer life. Attempting to come up with your own plan and your own way of doing things will always open the door for stress. It is so much easier to rely completely on God for wisdom, guidance, and direction as a leader.

3. Be intentional about taking time throughout your day and week for worship to God. There is liberty in cultivating a heart of thanksgiving to God for everything that you have in your life.

4. As a Christian leader you must learn the Biblical principle of casting the care to God. Remember that you are carrying out a specific assignment from God and He is helping you. It is unhealthy to carry the cares of life without getting a release from the pressures that come along with them. Contrary to what we have been programmed to believe, being stressed is not a sign that you are a good leader. It is a sign that you are a short-term leader.

5. Make a non-negotiable decision to take a vacation at least once or twice a year. Far too many leaders just work, work, work, and constantly burn themselves out without ever taking time away to rest and relax. When you incorporate a long weekend, or a vacation into your routine, it will help to keep you refreshed and stress-less.

All of these recommendations are lessons that I have learned and must continue to practice. I do believe that by continuing to make them a part of my life, it allows for me to recognize the symptoms of stress and what to do in order to become stress-less. The principles may appear to be simple and practical but implementing them will allow you to approach and respond to stress in the right way.

Don't forget to slow down to listen to your body and listen to your accountability circle of friends. None of the symptoms of stress such as agitation, fatigue, insomnia, loss of appetite, and anxiety have to take over your life. I want to also recommend that when things get overwhelming, find a counselor, and talk it out. Counseling is not just for people who have clinical health issues. Counseling is for those of us who may need to clear our minds from time to time in a safe manner.

Now that you have read this chapter and taken time to understand a little more about stress and its dangers, decide today to commit to living life as a leader in a healthy way.

Stress does not have to impact your life as a leader. Allow God to be a part of this special privilege as you lead others and commit to stay in the stress-less zone.

A PRAYER TO ASK JESUS TO BE YOUR SAVIOR:

*Dear God, I believe Jesus is your Son
and that He died for me,
and you raised Him from the grave.
Jesus, come into my heart.
I surrender every area of my life to
you forever. According to the
Bible I am Born Again.
Amen!*

APPLICATION TOOLS:

Examine all areas of your life for stress and be honest about how you are currently operating in your personal and professional leadership roles.

SELF-EXAM QUESTIONS

1. What is your definition of stress?

2. How have you dealt with stress in your life in the past?

3. Are there areas in your life or your position as a leader that you have allowed stress to creep in?

4. What is one thing that you can do today to release the pressure of stress in the area(s) that you have identified?

5. As a leader, will you be able to identify and assist team members who are dealing with stress in their own lives in a loving and efficient way?

GROUP DISCUSSION QUESTIONS

1. Do you have someone in your life as an accountability friend that will hold you to casting your cares over to God?

2. How easy is it for you to relax? If you do not have any hobbies, take the time today to ask God to show you how you can find that part of your life again. It's time to re-discover the kid in you.

3. How hard is it for you to commit your position as a leader completely to God to enjoy the liberty that comes only through your relationship with Him?

4. What areas in your life cause stress? How do you handle stress in those areas?

5. How will your organization or team benefit from you living in the stress-less zone?

Scriptures for Reflection: Matthew 11:28; Philippians 4:6-8; 1 Thessalonians 5:17; Psalms 55:17; 1 Peter 5:7; Matthew 6:34; Luke 10:40-41; John 14:27

CONVERSATIONS WITH GOD (NOTES):

Chapter 8

FORGIVENESS AFTER FAILURE

Come to Me, all you who labor and are heavy-laden and overburdened, and I will cause you to rest. I will ease and relieve and refresh your souls.

— *Matthew 11:28*

REFLECTIONS

Has there ever been a time in your life wherein you felt like the situation that you got yourself into was one from which you could never recover? Did it cause you to shut out friends and family members? Were there feelings of hopelessness and even fear? Were you faced with the possibility of losing your position as a leader? Maybe it was a company that folded before it even got off the ground. Regardless of what the perceived failure may have been in your life, at that moment did you feel that God had turned his back on you? How difficult was it to forgive yourself and see your way out? We can all relate to these feelings in one way or another. No matter what our view of failure may be, forgiveness is ours.

IT HAPPENS TO EVERYONE

Every one of us at some point in our lives has been in a situation where we felt like restoration was impossible. As a leader, whether it is failing at getting the desired contract for your company or handling an employee conflict the wrong way; forgiving yourself for the failure can linger on in your mind if not handled properly. Regardless of the source of our perceived failure, there are some things that we can consider when we find ourselves in this situation. Notice I said when we find ourselves in this situation, which means it can happen to all of us.

Let's take a moment to look at a couple of scenarios. The first scenario is when you recognize and acknowledge that you did not achieve your desired goal, you should immediately look for a way to regroup in order to move forward. By acknowledging that the plan did not work, it should allow you to recognize that this is an opportunity for restoration. Unfortunately, this is not what usually happens. In most cases, as a leader you will see the failure as the end of a dream with no way to move forward. An option could be to look at the situation as a chance to evaluate what went wrong and understand what could have been done differently. Unfortu-nately, some leaders will abandon the entire project. Does this sce-nario sound familiar?

The next scenario for us to consider is as a leader we make daily decisions for our teams and organizations. Many people put their trust in us to make the best decisions for them in the areas that we oversee. Let's say that you make a judgment call concerning the future of those you lead and the outcome is not favorable causing you to pay a very steep penalty. This failure may seem more difficult to rebound from because it is not just about business, it is personal in that it effects the lives of people.

As a leader when the decision touches the lives of those you lead in an intimate way, how do you normally respond? Here are a few ways that some leaders respond:

- A leader may look to blame others.
- ,A leader may question whether it was the best decision.
- A leader may take the decision as a personal failure.

How would you process this type of perceived failure?

THERE IS AN ANSWER

Do you know that the God who can restore a business failure is the same God that can restore a personal failure? There is no failure that is so difficult that God cannot bring us back to a place of healing and restoration in our professional and personal lives.

The first step in any restoration process is admitting that there is a problem and own our role in it. I understand that it may be uncomfortable for us to make the decision as to whether we are going to stay stuck in a place of guilt, shame, and condemnation; or will we press through the pain to return to a place of healing. The pain does not erase the purpose. If we choose to stay in the pain, we are not only limiting our lives in leadership, but we will never be able to witness all that God intended to do in and through us.

When we choose to wallow in self-pity about something that we feel is a failure, we must understand that our decision will limit those that we lead. I could say it this way, we are limiting those who are counting on us to demonstrate to them how to overcome a perceived failure. Just think we are leading when we feel we are succeeding, and we are leading how we respond when things don't go the way we plan. We also hinder our ability to walk in the freedom that is available to us by receiving God's forgiveness, restoration, and love which is available by His Grace. God is always the answer!

If you are currently a leader or going through a preparation process to become a leader, I want you to remember the things in your past that you felt were huge mistakes. Ask yourself did those things hinder you from your position today? God was the answer for your failure then and He is the answer today. We must decide to allow God to help us and then show us those areas where there is still more work to be done to allow us to continue to grow.

Do you recall when you needed to hear the right answer for a situation pertaining to your marriage, a purchase, a decision to relocate, or maybe even how to reorganize your team? Do you recall how you searched and put so much energy into making sure that the decision you made would be the right decision? As a leader you understand the importance of making sure that you are making the best decision possible for those that you lead. However, you may not consider that every answer that we need as a Christian leader has already been provided for us. God will always provide the answer before the problem shows up. I must give a disclaimer to this statement by saying that God's answer is available for things pertaining to or in line with His will for our lives. He is not obligated to give us the answers we think we should have if it does not line up with His will.

Would you say that succeeding in your role as a leader is the will of God? If you can say yes, then it should allow you to expect that if you pray and ask God for wisdom after a disappointment or a setback that the answer is already present.

> *"He restores my soul; He leads me in the paths of righteousness For His name's sake."*
> — Psalms 23:3

STARTING OVER

For some very successful leaders, the most difficult thing to do is to start over. It has been said that a setback is just an opportunity for a comeback. That statement shouts one thing – an attitude adjustment. Anytime we find ourselves experiencing what appears to be defeat, we cannot afford to continually focus on the setback. Our attitude really does affect our altitude. It is within the immediate stages of the disappointment that we have to implement the right thoughts to enable us to move forward. Remember we have to choose the right answer. We also must recognize that God will never leave us without aid or support, and He is a major factor in the journey to recovering from what appears to be failure.

I believe that the most important step in starting over may be connected to this word called forgiveness. Most of us have been forgiven or have been the one who needed to forgive someone else. Do you recall the first time you were faced with the decision to forgive someone who you believed disappointed you? Was it easy to face the pain and just decide to let the matter go, or better yet give it over to God? Well, that feeling that you experienced is pretty much the same experience that you encounter when you need to forgive yourself.

When you believe that you are the reason for your failures do you think about forgiveness as a part of the healing and restoration process? I can say that typically this is the furthest thing from most of our minds. It's easy for us to look for reasons outside of our own individual behavior to be the cause for our perceived failure. Let's say the failure came as a result of you being disobedient to what God told you to do, could you forgive yourself then? Even if your view of this failure was a result of you being over ambitious and getting out ahead of God's timing, you still must be willing to forgive yourself.

Oftentimes when it comes to the topic of forgiveness, we tend to think that it is based on how we feel. But forgiveness has nothing to do with our feelings. Forgiveness is a decision to rise above the situation and circumstances regardless of the emotional pressure to embrace the pain, hurt, or disappointment. These emotions will always move us away from what God has said to us and about us. Painful emotions that start with uncontrolled negative thoughts. You know those thoughts that tell you how you won't recover from this, or that you are worthless, that this is all your fault. Don't believe the lies! This set back is not the end, it's an opportunity to start over.

One of the things that I have observed in my own life as well as in the life of others is when it comes to forgiveness, it is sometimes easier to forgive someone else rather than to forgive ourselves. Could a reason be that we have the sense of feeling that we failed because we should have known better? Or maybe even thinking that we messed things up so bad that our leadership position can never be restored. Again, if you find yourself having these types of thoughts or feelings, cast them down immediately. The purpose of these thoughts and feelings is to try and exalt themselves above the truth of the Word of God. Negative thoughts of failure only serve to keep us stuck in the pain of the situation.

Your liberty as a leader rest in you implementing all of the tools shared throughout this book which will allow you to lead from a place of freedom. Getting stuck in failure is not one of those tools. If you find yourself in a place of not wanting to move forward, it's time to pick up the Bible and put your eyes on what God has already said about you and His plans for your life.

Once you fill your heart with what God says, then spend time in prayer listening for direction to pick yourself up and start again. The only way you fail is if you quit! Get back up and start again!

APPLICATION TOOLS:

Examine your heart to see how you are viewing failures in your life. Ask God to show you if you are holding on to any unforgiveness.

SELF-EXAM QUESTIONS

1. Did you allow a hurt or disappointment as a leader to cause you to feel like a failure?

2. Was your response to what you perceived to be a failure positive or negative?

3. Do you believe God was able to help you recover from your situation?

4. Have you experienced any battles in your thoughts after not seeing a positive outcome as a leader?

5. How difficult was it for you to regain your confidence in order to start over?

GROUP DISCUSSION QUESTIONS

1. Have you been able to recognize that God is still with you when you encounter a disappointment as a leader or in your personal life?

2. What was the hardest thing for you to do after feeling like you blew it as a leader?

3. Did you question your purpose when difficulties arose in your life as a leader?

4. How can you take the lessons you have learned through any setbacks and help disciple those that you lead?

5. How do you seek God after failure?

Scriptures for Reflection: Psalms 37:24; 1 Corinthians 10:13; Genesis 22:37-45; Job 1:42; Proverbs 3:4-5; Isaiah 40:31; Jeremiah 29:11; 1 Corinthians 12; Philippians 1:6; Psalms 138:8; Romans 11:29;1 Corinthians 15:1; Habakkuk 2:2-3. Psalms 23:3.

CONVERSATIONS WITH GOD (NOTES):

Chapter 9

JOY, THE KEY TO FINISHING YOUR RACE

"There has never been the slightest doubt in my mind that the God who started this great work in you would keep at it and bring it to a flourishing finish on the very day Christ Jesus appears."

— *Philippians 1:6*

READY, SET, GO

We have discussed various topics to help us to understand how to operate in liberty as a leader. The one thing that I hope you were able to grasp as you went through each chapter is the truth that God is the one who started us on our journey, and He is the one who will finish it. I believe we are all destined to operate in a specific purpose in our lives. I believe that we are called to lead. Leading does not start when you are positioned to lead a group of people, leading starts with leading oneself. The things that you have read throughout this book are all designed to allow you to do just that; lead yourself through awareness and balance.

Whether you are reading this book as a Christian or not, we each have been given a specific course to run in our lives. Pay attention to the things that you love and naturally excel in without much instruction. As you identify your gifts you can use them to change your areas of influence in leadership, family, friendships, and communities.

In that we go from level to level in the course of our careers and callings, we can look at our lives much like that of running in a race.

Have you ever paid attention to a relay race? If you notice, each person on the relay team has a specific assignment for their leg of the race. The runners are not positioned in the same lanes, nor are they positioned directly next to one another on the track. I would even guess that even though the training for the race may appear to be similar, they prepare for their specific leg of the race in slightly different ways. I would imagine that during the extensive training some days may be more difficult than others. For example, the days when the runner is tired or not running as fast as on other days, these are the days quitting comes to their mind.

Can you imagine after putting all of the hard work in and learning how to discipline their bodies by pressing through the long hours of training that they might come to a time in their career where they believe that they must quit? Runners experience injuries, personal changes, disappointments, setbacks, and victories all while preparing for the biggest event of their careers. These types of factors can have an effect on the runner's physical, mental, and emotional disposition as they prepare for the event.

Just take a moment and think through that example. I'm sure you can envision the process and preparation journey of a runner. The one thing I want each of us to see in thinking about the runner is that even though all of these elements may take place in the life of the runner, nothing compares with the joy that is evident as the athlete puts on the uniform and stands on the track to begin the race. It is pure excitement. The runner is no longer focused on the day-to-day ups and downs of getting to that point, the runner is focusing solely on the joy of crossing the finish line.

> *"Don't you realize that in a race everyone runs, but only one person gets the prize? So run to win!"*
>
> — 1 Corinthians 9:24

JOY, IS ON THE INSIDE

There is something powerful about the presence of joy. Joy is not based on a feeling because it exudes from the inside out. Unlike happiness which is totally dependent on situations and circumstances. Joy is a powerful tool that unleashes the ability to rise above any situation and move you from the back of the line directly to the front. The Bible says it's the joy of the Lord that gives us strength. I want you to think about that runner again. When the athlete is running their race with joy, it propels them to run faster without the thought of quitting. They are running their race, not the race of the runner to the left or the right. If the athlete focuses on the runner to the left or right of them, it will cause them to drift. This is true for us as well. When we take our eyes off God and stop operating in joy due to looking at what someone else is doing, we will drift off course in the race that God has ordained for our lives. It also has the potential to open the door for us to quit if we feel that we are no longer winning. Notice I never said the runner did not experience some challenging times. I drew our attention to the end of the runner's story and the goal of the runner rather than the things that could get him off course.

When we think about the topic of joy there are so many ideas about what it means and how to go about obtaining it. For corporate America leaders, joy is sometimes viewed as finally getting to the top executive position in the company or being able to get the high-rise corner office with the big window. How about in the church community? Joy could be viewed as being able to become the praise team leader; or being promoted to the position of pastor or department leader. In a dating relationship, joy can be viewed as finally finding Mr. or Mrs. Right. In a family joy could be having the first child. Regardless of what we believe joy may or may not be, wisdom for the Christian leader is to find out what God said about joy and the power that is available when we choose to operate in it on a daily basis. If you are not a Christian, these principles can still guide you towards obtaining joy in your future.

Typically, when we think about joy it is often confused with happiness. Happiness is always based on the circumstance. The evidence of whether I am happy or not is attached to how I feel about what is taking place. If I feel like everything is going well at the moment, or that I am doing a good job, then I see it as a place of happiness. Our happiness can also be determined by the sounds of what others are saying about us and to us. If we get all of the answers on a test and obtain a perfect score, we are happy. If we are included in a particular social circle because we check off all of the in-crowd boxes, we are happy. What if everyone in our department or organization constantly tells us that we are the best boss ever, I assure you we are happy.

The question then becomes if our happiness is based on our circumstance or what others are saying, then what happens as soon as the situation becomes unfavorable? Are we no longer happy? Could you imagine living life based on what others say or what is going on around you? I don't want to live life as if I am a yo-yo, always going up and down based on who is holding my strings. You and I do not have to function in that manner as leaders, we have something so powerful on the inside of us and it's called joy!

THE ROLLER COASTER RIDE

This may seem like a random question, but I assure you it is not. Have you ever taken a ride on a roller coaster? If it's your first time on you have no idea at what point during the ride that the drops or sharp turns will take place. There is a certain excitement that builds up if you love roller coasters and are a thrill seeker. If you are like me, you are holding on tight and closing your eyes to the point that they may need to be pried open because of being squinted so hard.

What I am attempting to get you to do is to look at your day as a leader from these two different perspectives. You can approach your day like the thrill seeker, looking forward to the drops and turns that may show up at work with the confidence of knowing that whatever shows up it will not steal your joy. Or you can be like me on the roller coaster, closing my eyes and holding on so tight that I completely miss the experience of riding a roller coaster.

My point is that every day we have the ability to choose joy no matter what situation we encounter. When we get up in the morning, we have to decide to choose joy. We have to decide that if something hits us unexpectedly that even though it may be painful, we are going to fight to keep our attitude in a place of joy. Life in general is unpredictable. It may be uncomfortable to deal with the drops and turns along the course that you are walking, especially if you are alone. If you feel like this describes you because there is not another person with you, I want you to know that as a child of God you will never be alone. God will always be with you. God will bring other individuals into your life to help you grow in joy. He will help you learn how to focus on the things that bring you joy. All that is required is an open mind and a willingness to adjust your perspective to see what God sees for your life.

SET THE STANDARD

Leadership can be very unpredictable. It requires strength, courage, wisdom, and most importantly the ability to genuinely care for those that you lead. It takes joy to lead others when whether they appreciate it or not. Remember, your joy is not tied to the assignment but rather to the One who is allowing you to be a leader. I know that some days you don't see anything to make you operate in joy, but we don't look for a reason before we decide to count it joy. I wonder how many days I have forfeited because I did not choose to count it joy. I'm sure I'm not the only one who can remember an event that stole my joy at work. If we can be honest, it probably was not something worthy of rehearsing over and over in our minds. These are lessons we learn as we grow as leaders and in our relationship with God. Wouldn't it be a great idea to not only learn the key to experiencing liberty in our role as leaders, but learn how to finish strong? Well, the secret key is operating in joy!

As a leader, we set the barometer for our departments and our organizations. The one thing that I have always appreciated about my favorite supermarket is their customer service. Joy is contagious! Have you ever visited an organization where you can see that all of the employees seem to be glad to work for the company?

Don't think for one minute their attitudes of joy are not intentional. This is a disposition that is taught and required for everyone on the team. I don't know about you, but I would rather work with a team that is full of joy than work with an organization that displays a disposition of gloom and doom.

When it comes to your area of influence, I would like to ask you to think about yourself for a moment, are you helping to spread joy to your team, or do you show more happiness where you lead? In my many years of working I've been on both sides of this lesson. During the times that I worked in an environment where joy was demonstrated within every area of the organization, I could not wait to wake up and start my day. When I worked with an organization wherein joy was not primary, I had to fight to remember and demonstrate this lesson that I am sharing with you. I will have joy and spread joy to all of those that I work with and for, regardless of what they choose to do.

> *I CHOOSE JOY!*

As we display a disposition of joy, our strength is built up and we are operating at maximum capacity. The effects of our joy are seen in the way we communicate with staff members and even in our productivity in leadership positions. Every relationship that we are blessed to have in life benefits from our decision to operate in joy. Joy is indeed an infectious character trait that we should desire to grow and operate in more frequently.

Let this last lesson on liberty in leadership cause you to renew your mind. The next time you desire to come up with a way to bring about change in your department, unit, organization, or family, stop for a moment, and consider starting with yourself as the leader. The first change that may need to take place is refill your joy level. After all it is the key to how you will finish your race and experience liberty in your role as a leader. Choose joy and make a positive impact on your family and this world!

APPLICATION TOOLS:

Examine your attitude towards your life and leadership. Ask God to show you any area in your life where you have lost your joy.

SELF-EXAM QUESTIONS

1. Are you still passionate about your purpose and assignment?

2. Is there something or someone that has caused you to lose your joy for your life and role as a leader?

3. What can you decide to do differently to activate joy in your life on a daily basis?

4. As a leader, what kind of attitude do you display on a consistent basis to those that you lead?

5. Will you trust your God given gift of joy to help you finish your race in leadership?

GROUP DISCUSSION QUESTIONS

1. Can you recall a time when your lack of joy impacted those in your family and workplace?

2. In what ways can you create an environment of joy within your department or organization?

3. How can you assist someone else who is lacking in their joy?

4. Are you able to release something or someone from your life that you feel is hindering you from operating in joy. Can you release it and the person today?

5. What are you willing to do to finish your race with joy?

Scriptures for Reflection: James 1:2; John 15:11; Proverbs 17:22; Psalms 16:11; Nehemiah 8:10; Galatians 5:22-23; 1 Corinthians 9:24

CONVERSATIONS WITH GOD (NOTES):

CONCLUSION

Liberty in leadership starts with our relationship with God and continues with our relationship with God. Whether or not we enjoy the blessing of fulfilling our assignment with ease depends on our willingness to rely on the Grace of God and the joy that resides in our hearts as His dear children.

There are so many examples of leadership styles available to us in this world. However, we can choose a different style of leading because as Christians we are different. We should be different in how we work, teach, lead, love and forgive those in our lives. God wants us to show those around us who do not know His way of doing things to learn them from His children as we lead.

I want to challenge you as a leader, whether in a corporate setting, in your home, or in ministry, to decide to lead based on God's plan for you as His leader. This may sound like a cute cliché, but I believe the things you do according to God's way will outlast all else. If you want to say at the end of your course as a leader that you were able to do it with good health and joy, then the information you have received in this book is a wonderful way to accomplish it.

May you experience the liberty that God has given you in your leadership and may you choose to help others lead from a place of health and peace for years to come!

ABOUT THE AUTHOR

Debra Jordan has a passion to help leaders carry out their assignments in a healthy manner. As a licensed and ordained minister for over 17 years, she has helped individuals and families heal from hurts, losses, and disappointments through counseling, teaching, and preaching. She holds a Doctor of Christian Counseling degree and has certifications as a Board Certified Professional and Pastoral Counselor and a Mental Health Coach with the American Association of Christian Counselors. She is also certified as an Anger Management Specialist I. She currently serves as Director of Impact Counseling. She and her husband reside in Florida with their two daughters.

CONVERSATIONS WITH GOD (NOTES):

CONVERSATIONS WITH GOD (NOTES):

CONVERSATIONS WITH GOD (NOTES):

CONVERSATIONS WITH GOD (NOTES):

CONVERSATIONS WITH GOD (NOTES):

CONVERSATIONS WITH GOD (NOTES):

Made in the USA
Monee, IL
25 August 2023